TERRYBERRY CHILDREN'S DEPARTMENT

OCEAN
Habitats

By **Paul Bennett**

GARETH**STEVENS**
PUBLISHING
A Member of the WRC Media Family of Companies

Please visit our web site at: www.garethstevens.com
For a free color catalog describing Gareth Stevens Publishing's
list of high-quality books and multimedia programs,
call 1-800-542-2595 or 1-800-387-3178 (Canada).
Gareth Stevens Publishing's fax: (414) 332-3567.

Library of Congress Cataloging-in-Publication Data

Bennett, Paul, 1954-
  Ocean habitats / Paul Bennett. – North American ed.
     p. cm. — (Exploring habitats)
  Includes bibliographical references and index.
  ISBN-10: 0-8368-7255-X – ISBN-13: 978-0-8368-7255-2 (lib. bdg.)
  1. Marine biology—Juvenile literature.   2. Ocean—Juvenile literature.
I. Title. II. Series.
QH91.16.B47   2006
578.77'7—dc22   2006044331

This North American edition first published in 2007 by
Gareth Stevens Publishing
A Member of the WRC Media Family of Companies
330 West Olive Street, Suite 100
Milwaukee, WI 53212 USA

This U.S. edition copyright © 2007 by Gareth Stevens, Inc. Original
edition copyright © 2002 by ticktock Entertainment Ltd. First published
in Great Britain in 1999 by ticktock Publishing Ltd., Unit 2, Orchard
Business Centre, North Farm Road, Tunbridge Wells, Kent, TN2 3XF.

Gareth Stevens editor: Richard Hantula
Gareth Stevens designer: Charlie Dahl
Gareth Stevens managing editor: Mark J. Sachner
Gareth Stevens art direction: Tammy West
Gareth Stevens production: Jessica Morris

Picture Credits: t=top, b=bottom, c=centre, l=left, r=right, OFC=outside
front cover, OBC=outside back cover, IFC=inside front cover

AKG Photo; 3rb. B&C Alexander Photography; 2l, 2c, 2/3t, 3tl, 4tl, 4/5
(main pic), 5c, 6tl, 7br, 7bl, 8bl, 8/9b, 8/9c, 9br, 10bl, 10tl, 10cr, 12/13b + 32,
12/13c, 14/15 (main pic), 15tr, 15cr, 16l, 18br, 18cl, 18tc, 18/19t, 22tl,
22/23b, 23c, 23tr, 24tl, 24c, 25cr, 25tl, 25/26 (main pic), 25/26c, 26tr, 28bc,
28bl, 28tl, 29bl, 29br, 29c, 29tl, 30l, 30/31bc, 31cl, 31tr. Oxford Scientific
Films; 3tr, 5tr, 6tr, 8c, 8l, 11r, 11tl, 13br, 14/15c, 16c, 18cr, 19tc, 20tl, 21br,
21tr, 21tl, 21rc, 24bl, 24/25c, 25tr, 31br. Planet Earth Pictures; IFC, 3cl, 9tl,
9tr, 10/11c, 12t, 12b, 13tr, 13rc, 14tl, 16/17b, 17cl, 17tl, 17tr, 19b, 20/21c,
20/21b, 23tl, 30cl. Survival Anglia; 12c.

Every effort has been made to trace the copyright holders and we apologize in
advance for any unintentional omissions. We would be pleased to insert the
appropriate acknowledgement in any subsequent edition of this publication.

Printed in the United States of America

1 2 3 4 5 6 7 8 9 10 09 08 07 06

CONTENTS

LOOKING FOR A MEAL

The spiny lobster (*left*) scavenges
for food in the rocky coastal
regions of the world. It is a
relative of the ordinary lobster,
but has large antennae and spines
instead of claws.

UNDER THE OCEAN

L ife can be found everywhere in the oceans, from the shallow, sunlit upper waters to the darkest depths. This makes the oceans by far the largest habitat in our world. They cover most of the Earth's surface, yet they are mostly unexplored because of their sheer vastness and power. The frightening sea monsters that early sailors claimed had attacked their ships were certainly flights of fancy. But as you will discover, there are certainly monstrous-looking creatures living in the salty depths. The oceans teem with life. Some sea creatures are tiny. For example, you would need a microscope to see phytoplankton (tiny algae and other microorganisms that are capable of photosynthesis and that form the basis of most life in the oceans). Others are huge – the blue whale is the largest known creature that ever lived. It can grow to more than 100 feet (30 meters) and can weigh over 150 tons. It is now an endangered species due to overhunting in the past.

NOT JUST A FRIENDLY FACE

The bottlenose dolphin (*left*) seems to have a knowing smile on its face. It is a very intelligent animal, able to "talk" to others of its kind with a wide range of grunts, whistles, and clicks. Dolphins, like whales, are not fish but mammals, which means they feed their young on milk.

WEIRD AND WONDERFUL

The leafy sea dragon (*left*) is just one of the odd-looking creatures of the oceans. It is, in fact, a type of sea horse, which is a small fish. Although it is a poor swimmer, it is well adapted to its life in the beds of seaweed that grow in shallow waters around Australia. The array of leaflike flaps along its body act as camouflage, making it hard for a predator to spot it among seaweeds.

PLANET OCEAN

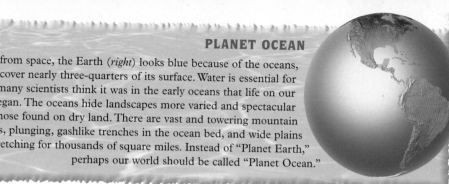

Viewed from space, the Earth (*right*) looks blue because of the oceans, which cover nearly three-quarters of its surface. Water is essential for life; many scientists think it was in the early oceans that life on our planet began. The oceans hide landscapes more varied and spectacular than those found on dry land. There are vast and towering mountain ranges, plunging, gashlike trenches in the ocean bed, and wide plains stretching for thousands of square miles. Instead of "Planet Earth," perhaps our world should be called "Planet Ocean."

SPEED AND POWER

A black marlin leaps high out of the water (*left*). The fish's power and shape make it one of the fastest swimmers in the ocean. Its snout extends into a sharp spike, helping it cut through the water with little resistance, and its streamlined body tapers gently until it meets the curved tail. To feed, it dives into shoals of fish, attacking them at high speed with remarkable precision.

GENTLE GIANT

Despite its size the humpback whale (*right*) is harmless to humans. Humpbacks grow as long as 50 feet (15 m) and may weigh as much as 45 tons, but they are graceful swimmers, using their large flippers to move their huge bulk with ease. They are baleen whales. That is, they lack teeth; instead, comblike structures of a substance called baleen hang from the upper jaw and act as a strainer, trapping food, such as small fish or krill, when the whale expels a huge mouthful of water.

UNDERWATER GARDENS

Coral reefs teem with life (*right*). They grow only in warm water that is clean and shallow and has sufficient light. The majority of reefs are found in the tropics, in regions where there is a rocky platform not too far below the surface. Many fish that live among the corals have flat bodies, which allow them to swim into, or through, the reef's many cracks and crevices.

OCEANS OF THE WORLD

Traditionally, four oceans were recognized – the Pacific, Atlantic, Indian, and Arctic. Many experts now regard the southernmost parts of the first three as a separate Southern Ocean. The oceans are all connected, forming a single, large mass of salt water. They are also joined to seas, which cover smaller areas and are shallower. The Mediterranean Sea between Europe and Africa, for example, is linked to the Atlantic by the Strait of Gibraltar. The oceans affect the weather and climate, and ocean currents influence the movement of plankton and large marine animals. The oceans are themselves afffected by the Sun and Moon, whose gravity causes the tides.

THE ATLANTIC OCEAN

The Atlantic Ocean (*above*) is the second largest ocean in the world. It separates North and South America in the west from Europe and Africa in the east. A current called the Gulf Stream carries warm water from the tropics northward to the region of Norway, where it keeps the sea from freezing. Underneath the ocean is a vast mountain range called the Mid-Atlantic Ridge, which is longer than the Himalayas.

THE PACIFIC OCEAN

The Pacific (*right*) is the largest and deepest of the oceans, with an area roughly double that of the Atlantic. "Pacific" means peaceful, but this ocean actually has some of the most violent sea and weather conditions in the world, including fierce tropical storms and destructive tsunamis (powerful waves caused by a volcano eruption, earthquake, or landslide on the ocean floor).

THE SOUTHERN OCEAN

Formed by the southern reaches of the Pacific, Atlantic, and Indian Oceans, the Southern Ocean surrounds Antarctica, the snow- and ice-covered location of the South Pole. The rich, chilly water supports a wide variety of life, such as the crabeater seal (*left*), which has jagged teeth that it uses like a sieve to strain krill – the small, shrimplike creatures on which it feeds – from the water.

THE ARCTIC OCEAN

The Arctic is a partly frozen ocean that lies to the north of North America, Asia, and Europe. In the summer months much of the pack ice melts, reducing the area covered by sea ice. In addition, great chunks of ice plunge into the sea from the ends of glaciers around Greenland and float away as towering icebergs (*left*).

ARCTIC
OCEAN

ARCTIC
OCEAN

PACIFIC
OCEAN

ATLANTIC
OCEAN

PACIFIC
OCEAN

INDIAN
OCEAN

SOUTHERN OCEAN

ARCTIC OCEAN
Area: 5,400,000 sq miles (14,000,000 sq km)
Av. depth: 4,100 feet (1,250 m)
ATLANTIC OCEAN
Area: 30,000,000 sq miles (77,000,000 sq km)
Av. depth: 13,000 feet (4,000 m)
INDIAN OCEAN
Area: 26,500,000 sq miles (68,600,000 sq km)
Av. depth: 13,000 feet (4,000 m)
PACIFIC OCEAN
Area: 60,000,000 sq miles (155,000,000 sq km)
Av. depth: 13,780 feet (4,200 m)
SOUTHERN OCEAN
Area: 7,800,000 sq miles (20,300,000 sq km)
Av. depth: 13-16,000 feet (4-5,000 m)
(rounded figures)

THE INDIAN OCEAN

The Indian Ocean is an ocean of extremes. Its climate ranges from warm and tropical in the north to icy-cold where it meets the waters of the Southern Ocean. Dotted across the Indian Ocean are groups of beautiful islands, such as Kaafu Atoll (*right*) in the Maldives, a string of coral islands to the southwest of India.

LAYERS OF LIFE

FLYING FISH

Flying fish (*above*) can be found in the open ocean. They can generate enough speed underwater to leap out of the water and, using their winglike fins, glide through the air for 30 seconds or more to escape enemies.

Scientists divide the oceans into broad layers, or zones, so that if you took a trip down to the bottom of the ocean in a submersible (a type of deep-diving submarine) you would see the sunlit upper waters giving way to the twilight zone at about 650 feet (200 m). Here the waters are poorly lit – too little light for photosynthesis – and the temperature of the water drops rapidly. Below 3,300 feet (1,000 m) or so you would be in the dark zone, where no light penetrates from above. The ocean floor is mostly a flat, deep "abyssal" plain ("abyssal" literally means "bottomless"). The deepest areas are creases in the ocean floor called trenches. The deepest known point, 35,840 feet (10,924 m) below sea level, is at the bottom of the Mariana Trench in the western Pacific.

IN THE TWILIGHT ZONE

Below the shallow waters are the shady depths of the twilight zone. Life is less common here compared to the sunlit upper waters, but still generally more abundant than the blackness of the deep ocean. Types of animals found here, such as sponges (*right*), can also be seen at other depths. Sponges are not free-swimming but are attached to the same spot nearly all of their lives. Creatures such as these are called sessile animals.

IN SHALLOW WATERS

Whether near the shore or out in the open ocean, animals and plants are most abundant in the well-lit shallow depths (*below*).

THE DEEP OCEAN

Despite the absence of light, the bottom of the deep ocean is not lifeless. At some spots on the ocean floor communities of organisms exist based on special forms of bacteria that are "chemosynthetic" – capable of making food from chemicals. They are found, for example at places on the bottom of the Pacific, Atlantic, and Indian Oceans where vents spew out from below hot water that is rich in chemicals. In one such community (*above*), the brown-looking material is made up of chemosynthetic bacteria, which serve as food for tube worms (the white animals) and other creatures.

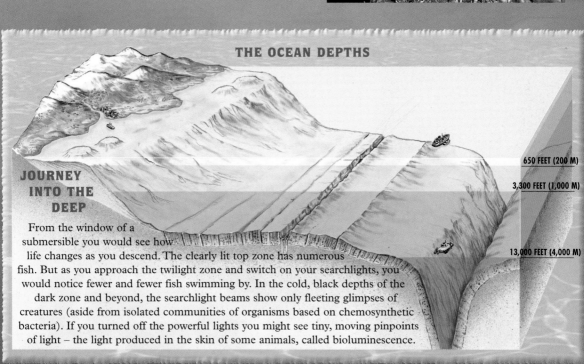

THE OCEAN DEPTHS

650 FEET (200 M)

3,300 FEET (1,000 M)

13,000 FEET (4,000 M)

JOURNEY INTO THE DEEP

From the window of a submersible you would see how life changes as you descend. The clearly lit top zone has numerous fish. But as you approach the twilight zone and switch on your searchlights, you would notice fewer and fewer fish swimming by. In the cold, black depths of the dark zone and beyond, the searchlight beams show only fleeting glimpses of creatures (aside from isolated communities of organisms based on chemosynthetic bacteria). If you turned off the powerful lights you might see tiny, moving pinpoints of light – the light produced in the skin of some animals, called bioluminescence.

IN SUNLIT WATERS

T he upper regions of the oceans are full of life. Here sunlight is able to penetrate the water, providing the essential energy that plants and other photosynthetic organisms need to change the chemicals in the seawater into food. With the exception of communities of organisms on the ocean floor based on chemosythentic bacteria, the basis of the food chain for all life within the oceans is phytoplankton – microscopic algae and other very tiny photosynthetic organisms that bloom in the sunlit waters. These are grazed on by tiny animals called zooplankton, which, in turn, are food for larger animals.

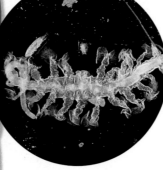

ZOOPLANKTON

Huge numbers of zooplankton (*above*) float among the phytoplankton. These tiny animals are joined by the larvae of crabs and lobsters, as well as mollusks, small shrimps, and swimming crabs. They feed on phytoplankton, on each other, or both. This whole drifting collection of living things is called plankton. It forms a rich soup on which many creatures depend for their survival.

FLOATING RAFTS OF WEED

Great yellowish rafts of sargassum weed (*above*), buoyed up by its small air bladders, can be seen in the Sargasso Sea in the Atlantic Ocean. The weed originally comes from weed beds in shallow, tropical waters. But during storms it floats out into the open ocean. Soon it begins to attract a wide variety of creatures.

JELLYFISH

Jellyfish are invertebrates – creatures without a backbone. The compass jellyfish (*left*) floats near the surface of the ocean, often in large, wind-drifted groups near the coast. Its long tentacles have stings for catching fish and other animals that stray into them. Some jellyfish are well known for their powerful stings. For example, the box jellyfish of Australia can kill a person in less than five minutes. As a defense against the stings, Australian lifeguards used to wear outsize women's tights pulled up over their bodies.

WIDE-MOUTHED FISH

The manta ray's diet of plankton is so nourishing that it can grow to an incredible 23 feet (7 m) across and weigh up to 1.5 tons. On either side of its head are flipperlike scoops that channel the food into its wide mouth (*right*). The plankton are caught on combs as the water leaves its throat through slits on the sides of its head.

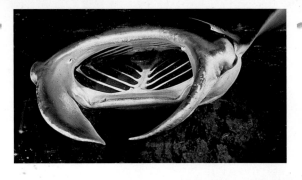

PARROT FISH

A regal parrot fish nips off pieces of coral using its sharp, beaklike teeth (*above*) and then grinds up the hard mouthful with its back teeth to extract the coral polyps – the small creatures largely responsible for the creation of the reef. Coral reefs are famed for their abundance of colorful fish. The bright hues make the fish stand out when they swim around the reef, but colors are good camouflage when they dive for safety among the corals.

HEADS UP

Garden eels live in the huge expanses of sand that cover the ocean floor near the edges of continents. They bury their tails in the sand and, with their heads held up (*above*), feed on particles of food carried in the currents that sweep across the sand.

PACKED TOGETHER

A shoal of sardines feeds on a living broth of plankton (*left*). These and other small fish, such as herring, anchovies, and flying fish, are hunted by marine predators, including mackerel, that are only slightly bigger than their prey. By swimming together the sardines follow one another in their search for food-rich waters. Large shoals make it difficult for hunters to choose which fish to attack first.

THE TWILIGHT ZONE

SPONGES

These sponges (*above*) live on the ocean bottom. They filter out food particles by drawing in water through small pores and passing it out through larger holes. Food becomes scarcer and scarcer the deeper you go. With so little nourishment available, it can take a long time for deeper-dwelling animals to grow to full maturity.

The further you descend, the darker and colder the oceans get. The light fades rapidly, and soon it becomes close to freezing. Algae and other photosynthetic microorganisms do not grow here, so food is scarce. But there is a steady rain of debris – the bodies of creatures and droppings – drifting slowly downward from the surface, and this provides a ready meal for the zooplankton, shrimp, and fish living in the twilight zone of the ocean. Many creatures have developed large eyes so that they can see in the dim light, and their bodies are often colored red, drab brown, or black, providing excellent camouflage in the gloom. Most creatures also produce their own light, generated by light-producing organs called photophores. Sometimes the lights are on the underside of their bodies so that the creatures are less visible. Some animals spend the hours of daylight in the safety of the twilight zone but come up to shallower waters to feed at night.

DAGGER TOOTHED

The viperfish's mouth (*left*) has daggerlike teeth for grabbing prey. The lower jaw is bigger than the top jaw, because the bottom teeth are so long – in fact, they do not fit into the mouth when it is closed. The fish has light organs, or photophores, which it uses to lure prey. The jaws hinge open very wide to allow the fish to swallow its meal.

SQUID

Torpedo-shaped squid are among the most common creatures living in the sea. This one (*below*) has organs along its body to light its way in the deep water. Because of the huge pressure exerted by the water on the bodies of creatures that live far below the surface, many of them are small. However, there are exceptions: the giant squid, which lives as deep as 3,300 feet (1,000 m), is thought to grow up to 66 feet (20 m) long.

SEA LILY

The crinoid, or sea lily, might look like a plant. In fact, it is an animal. Its delicate "leaves" are feathery arms encircling the mouth. This one (*right*) is on a shallow coral reef, but others are found at much greater depths, living in the deep sea and trenches.

BOGGLE EYES AND WIDE MOUTH

The hatchetfish gets its name from the fact that its deep belly gives it the appearance of a small ax. Its bulbous eyes (*left*) are specially designed for seeing in poor light; they are many times more sensitive to light than the human eye. Some hatchetfish look upward, hoping to see the outline of their prey against the light from above, and then catch it in their wide mouth. In this hatchetfish (*right*), the bones are stained red so you can see the skeleton.

THE DEEP OCEAN

No light from the Sun ever reaches below 3,300 feet (1,000 m). Consequently, the deep ocean is completely black. Much of the rain of debris is eaten higher up, and so there is hardly any food – which is why there are fewer animals at the greater depths. The abyssal plain, down to about 20,000 feet (6,000 m), is covered in a layer of ooze. This mudlike carpet can be very thick – hundreds of yards in some places – and is very soft. Scattered on some parts of the ocean floor are nodules – hard, round lumps of minerals, such as manganese, nickel, and iron. Some are the size of cherries; others are as large as grapefruits. The nodules are not washed there by currents but form in very deep water. The nodules are valuable and humans have tried to extract them by dredging, but the process is costly.

FISH WITH STILTS

The tripod fish (*above*) has a special adaptation for its life at the bottom of the ocean – long stilts for standing or moving across the ooze. The thin stilts are like stiff filaments – one on each of its fins and one on its tail fin, making a tripod – which help the fish stay clear of the soft ooze on the bottom of the ocean and move along without stirring up clouds of particles. The fish also has long antennae to help it "see" in the dark.

MOUTH FOR GULPING

The gulper eel (*left*) lives up to its name. To catch its prey, it swims slowly through the inky blackness with its gaping mouth wide open. When it runs into a small fish or shrimp, it immediately snaps its mouth shut and gulps down its prey before the prey has time to escape.

ANGLERFISH

This ferocious-looking fish (*right*) with sharp teeth and a wide gape attracts prey with a bioluminiscent lure, located on a long spine on the top of its head. If another fish is foolish enough to think the lure is food and comes near, the anglerfish quickly sucks it up whole into its large mouth. A female anglerfish is up to 20 times larger than the male fish. In order to mate, the small male uses his teeth to attach himself to the female's body close to her reproductive opening. His body begins to fuse with her body, and eventually his heart wastes away as his bloodstream is replaced by hers. He is unable to swim away and is attached forever, fertilizing her eggs for the rest of her life.

DELICATE BASKET

The fragile Venus's-flower-basket sponge has an intricate skeleton (*left*). The sponge, which may grow as long as 12 inches (30 centimeters), lives in colonies on the bottom of the ocean.

BRITTLE STARFISH

Brittle starfish (*right*) are found crawling on the bottom of both shallow and deep waters. Their arms are thin and very fragile and easily break off, hence their name. However, the starfish is able to grow new arms. It uses its arms to collect food fragments drifting by.

RATTAIL FISH

This little fish (*left*) gets its name from its long, thin body and tail. Fish living at great depths are often small and delicate. One reason for their small size is the scarcity of food and nutrients needed for growth. The rattail fish lives well below the strong ocean currents, in regions where the water is still, and so it has little need for a powerful body for swimming. Hence it has developed its characteristic long, tail-like shape.

SEA CUCUMBER

Sea cucumbers (*left and below*) are sluglike animals that live in both deep and shallow waters. They crawl along the bottom of the seas and oceans, munching their way through the sediment in a quest for particles of food. Some deep-sea cucumbers have long tube feet to help them walk through the soft ooze.

IN THE DARK

COLORED GLASS

Seemingly glasslike jellyfish can be found drifting in all the oceans of the world, from the sunlit surface waters down to the twilight zone. An example (*above*) is *Aglantha digitale*, which offers a striking display of rainbow colors. It has a transparent body shaped like a dome, and an opening that takes in food and passes out waste.

T he deep ocean is a very inhospitable place: no sunlight, icy-cold temperatures, a scarcity of food, and a water pressure so great it would crush in an instant any diver who dared to go that deep. The animals that live at such depths have special adaptations to allow them to survive the harsh conditions. For example, many deep-sea predators have massive mouths for catching prey (often several times larger than themselves) and stomachs that can stretch to take the huge meals. This is necessary because encounters between animals at great depths are few, and every opportunity for a meal must be taken, however large.

A FEROCIOUS BITE

The wicked-looking teeth of this deep-sea fish (*left*) are not for ripping massive chunks out of its prey. Instead, they are for trapping an unfortunate fish inside its cavernous mouth. The teeth are bent backward, allowing a fish to pass easily into the mouth. If the prey is very large – perhaps even larger than the predator – the mouth might not be able to close properly. Then the teeth act as a barrier, preventing the luckless prey from escaping.

16

NATURAL LIGHT

In the deep, dark depths the only natural light you will see is from the creatures that live there. In nearly all cases the glow comes from the photophores in their bodies (*above*). The fact that so many animals of the deep have these light producing organs shows that light plays a crucial role in their survival. The lights can be used to attract or locate prey or a mate, or to confuse an enemy. Common sites for the organs are on the side of the head, on the flank, on the underside of the body, and on the end of a fin ray.

HAPPY-GO-LUCKY

Because of their large mouths and strange shape, many of the carnivorous fish found in the deep look extremely odd (*left*). Below the twilight zone, few fish have swim bladders (air-filled sacs that allow fish to regulate their buoyancy, so that when they stop swimming they neither sink nor float upward). Instead, deep-ocean fish achieve "neutral buoyancy," largely by having thin, lightweight skeletons and muscles. They are small, too – many no more than 4 inches (10 cm) long. In the tremendous pressure of the still water they appear to hover when not swimming.

SCARLET SHRIMP

Where a tiny amount of light still reaches the depths, shrimps are deep red in color (*right*). In the sunlit waters, their color would make them stand out and they would be easy prey for a hungry fish. But in the lower reaches of the twilight zone, the redness of the shrimp's body is effective camouflage; in the dim light, red appears black, so that the shrimp blends into the background. Below the twilight zone shrimps are nearly colorless – the blanket of blackness hides them from their predators and so there is no need for camouflage.

UNDERSEA GARDENS

FAN WORM

Many marine animals look rather like plants, and the fan worm (*above*) is one of them. It uses the tentacles of the fan to ensnare particles of food drifting in the water.

I n the sunlit waters of the oceans grow "gardens" of seaweed. Seaweed is, in fact, algae. On land, algae grow in damp or wet areas and are small. In the oceans microscopic algae make up a major part of phytoplankton. But algae also take on larger forms – seaweed. Many seaweeds have structures resembling land plants, but because their stipe (stem) and fronds (leaves) are supported by the water, some types grow to enormous sizes. Most seaweeds anchor themselves to rock by rootlike "holdfasts," which grow into cracks in the rock. The holdfasts prevent them from being carried away by the waves. Seaweeds are home to a large array of creatures, including fish, crabs, shrimps, and sea urchins.

THE COW OF THE SEA

Dugongs (*below*) are also called sea cows, because they graze on the sea grasses growing in the warm, shallow waters of the Indian and Pacific Oceans. They can be as long as 12 feet (3.6 m). They are the only vegetarian sea mammals and are very shy. Some people think that dugongs may have been the origin of mermaid legends. When viewed from a distance by early sailors, it is said, dugongs may have looked humanlike.

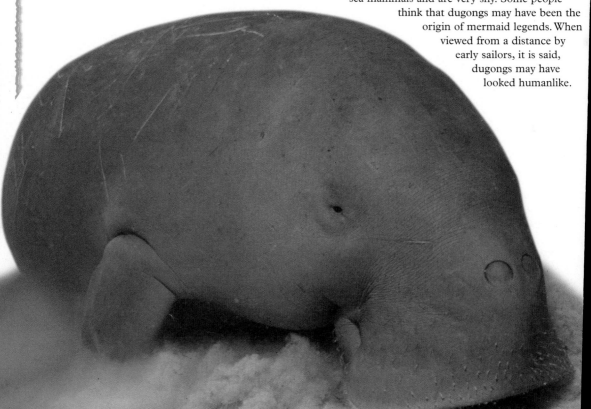

SEAWEED ZONES

Like plants on land, seaweeds need light in order to grow. Because of this they are found only in sunlit waters. The color of seaweeds gives an indication of their depth. Near the surface grow bright green seaweeds, such as sea lettuce (*right*). Then come greenish-brown seaweeds, such as the wracks, followed by brown kelp and then the red seaweeds.

ALL WRAPPED UP

The sea otter (*left*) is a familiar inhabitant of the kelp beds of the Pacific coast of North America, where the animals dive for food, such as shellfish, crustaceans, and sea urchins. After bringing the food to the surface, the sea otter, using a stone as an anvil, repeatedly bashes the shell until it cracks open, exposing the tasty flesh inside. When a sea otter wants to sleep, it rolls over and over in kelp until the seaweed is wrapped around its body. The kelp stops it from drifting away on the tide or with the wind.

KELP FORESTS

This diver (*right*) is swimming through a forest of kelp off the coast of California. The large brown seaweeds, found in cold seas, may grow more than 200 feet (60 m) long, providing shelter for the animals that live among them. Unlike land plants, kelp and other seaweeds have no need for roots; they are able to absorb all the water and nutrients they need from the water around them. Instead of roots they may have a holdfast, whose function is simply to attach the seaweed to the rock.

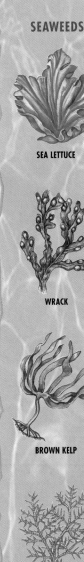

SEAWEEDS

SEA LETTUCE

WRACK

BROWN KELP

RED SEAWEED

CORAL REEFS

Coral reefs are found in warm, clear waters, mainly in tropical regions. A primary role in the creation of reefs is played by coral polyps, small anemone-like creatures that filter the water for food. Each polyp builds itself a protective outer skeleton to live in, made of calcium carbonate (or limestone). As it grows, it develops a filament from which sprouts another polyp, which also builds a protective skeleton for itself. Gradually, the reef grows upward and outward, the outer layer being made of living coral growing on the skeletons of dead members of the colony. Living within the polyp are tiny algae, which are essential for the polyps' growth. The algae depend on sunlight for photosynthesis, so coral reefs do not grow below about 500 feet (150 m). Many creatures make their homes in or on the reef, creating one of the richest wildlife communities found anywhere in nature.

HARD AND SOFT

There are both hard corals, made by polyps with a hard outer skeleton, and soft corals, built by polyps with a hard internal skeleton (*left*). The strange shapes of reef corals give rise to some equally strange names: staghorn, brain, sea fan, dead-man's-fingers, and organ-pipe coral, for example. Corals come in many different colors. Hard corals, such as staghorn, are white because of their hard outer skeletons. But the soft corals are often brightly colored yellow, red, green, black, or blue.

HARD CORAL   SOFT CORAL

CROWN OF THORNS

The large, spiky-looking red starfish called crown of thorns (*right*) feeds on coral polyps. It does a great deal of damage and has destroyed large areas of Australia's Great Barrier Reef.

DEADLY BEAUTY

The lionfish (*below*) may be attractive, but it is one of the most poisonous creatures in the ocean. Its lacy spines house venom that can leave nasty and painful wounds. The fish's splendid display serves as a warning to predators not to tamper with it.

REEF BUILDING

Erskine Island Reef (*above*) is part of the Great Barrier Reef, which stretches for 1,400 miles (2,300 kilometers) along the northeast coast of Australia. It was built by creatures the size of a pinhead over a period of several million years. The small, low island, called a cay, is made up of fragments of coral. In the Pacific, reefs often form a ring around volcanic islands. These are called fringing reefs. Water enclosed by a reef is called a lagoon. Atolls are circular reefs or strings of coral islands surrounding a lagoon.

RECORD BREAKER

The mollusk with the largest shell is the giant Tridacna clam (*above*). This giant, filter-feeding creature can grow up to 5 feet (1.5 m) wide and weigh as much as a quarter of a ton. It is one of the largest invertebrates, or animals without a backbone.

TINY TENTACLES

Coral polyps have tentacles with which to catch plankton. The tentacles, which form rings around the mouth of the animal, have darts that sting their prey. During the day, the stalks of the polyps are retracted into the protective skeletons, making the coral look like dead rock. At night they spread their tentacles to feed (*left*).

GREAT WHITE SHARK

TUNA

ANCHOVIES

ZOOPLANKTON

PHYTOPLANKTON

At the top of the principal marine food chain are the large hunters, such as sharks. These eat large fish, which catch smaller fish, which in turn rely on zooplankton. The zooplankton eat phytoplankton. Therefore the tiny organisms that make food through photosynthesis are the basis of most life in the oceans.

PREDATORS AND PREY

The deadly game of attack and defense is played out at every level of the ocean. Creatures are constantly on the lookout for prey. But there is no such thing as an easy meal. No creature – however large or small – wants to end up as lunch for another animal. Some animals, such as the poisonous lionfish, have bright warning colors that tell a predator to keep clear of its poisonous spines. But other animals must take evasive action if they are to survive an attack.

JET POWERED

Scallops have a unique way of escaping the deadly clutches of a hungry starfish (*above*). They use jet power to launch themselves off the bottom of the ocean, and swim away by squeezing a jet of water out of their shells. Unlike most other mollusks of their type, scallops do not bury themselves in the sand or attach themselves to the rocky seabed, and so they are able to escape a marauding predator.

NO ESCAPE

Even the stinging cells on the tentacles of the jellylike *Porpita* are no defense against the sea slug *Glaucus*, a type of shell-less mollusk (*left*). The sea slug crawls along the underside of the water surface looking for *Porpita*, and when it finds one, it immediately starts feeding on it, stings and all.

DEADLY EMBRACE

The flowerlike sea anemone (*right*), with its colorful "petals," looks pretty and innocent. But any small fish that comes too close must beware: the petals are armed with poisonous stinging cells. Once caught in its deadly embrace, the poor fish is pulled toward the anemone's mouth in the center of the ring of tentacles.

UNDERWATER FLIGHT

Many seabirds dive into the water to catch a meal, but the Galapagos penguin (*left*) chases fish underwater, using its flipperlike wings to propel it rapidly through the water. When fish swim in shoals, they may confuse the bird, preventing it from deciding on a catch. The flashing of their silvery bodies may also stun the penguin for a moment, allowing the fish to escape.

KILLER ON THE ATTACK

On an Argentinian beach (*right*) a killer whale, or orca, attacks sea lions by charging at them in shallow water. An air-breathing mammal, it is willing to almost beach itself in order to catch its prey. Orcas can grow as long as 33 feet (10 m). They belong to the dolphin family in the cetacean (whale) group and are the only known cetacean to prey on whales.

TERROR OF THE OCEANS

The most feared fish in the ocean is the great white shark (*below*). This eating machine prefers seals, turtles, and large fish, but occasionally has attacked humans, its sharp teeth leaving terrible injuries. The shark's streamlined body allows it to swim effortlessly through the water, driven by its large, powerful tail. Unlike many other fish, sharks lack a swim bladder to provide buoyancy, so they must swim constantly to stay afloat.

MIGRATION

SHRIMP LARVAE

The shrimp *Parapandalus* (*above*) lives at depths of about 1,640-2,300 feet (500-700 m) in the dim regions of the ocean. The female carries her eggs stuck to her legs on the underside of her body. When the eggs hatch, the larvae swim up to the surface to feed on phytoplankton. As they grow, they change their diet and start to eat other small animals. The larvae eventually migrate down to the depths where the adults live.

nimals that move from one place to another are said to migrate. For example, in the ocean zooplankton make a daily migration. During the night they feed on phytoplankton that live in the surface waters. But as day breaks they swim down several hundred yards to escape hungry predators. However, for many other marine animals migration is more commonly associated with breeding. Some fish, seals, whales, and turtles make spectacular migrations, often swimming thousands of miles on difficult journeys to lay their eggs or give birth to their offspring. They travel to a place where the young have the best chance of survival, perhaps because of plentiful food supplies, and they are guided on their journey by ocean currents.

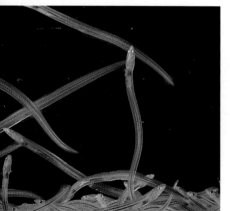

MIGRATION MYSTERY

The breeding habits of the European eel (*left*) remained a mystery until the 20th century. Then it was discovered that the adult eels leave the rivers of Europe and swim out into the Sargasso Sea in the Atlantic Ocean, where they spawn (produce eggs) and then die. The larvae drift back to Europe along the Gulf Stream. After about three years, now young eels, or elvers, they arrive at the rivers, where they remain until they, too, are ready to return to the spawning grounds in the Atlantic.

THE CONGER EEL

The conger eel (*right*) of the North Atlantic is a fearless hunter. It has rows of sharp, backward-pointing teeth that grip into its prey. The only known spawning ground of the conger eel is north of the Azores. It seems that all Western European congers travel here in midsummer to lay their eggs, later returning to colder northern waters.

WHALE OF A TIME

The feeding grounds of the southern right whale (*left*) are the food-rich waters of the Southern Ocean. When it is time for the females to give birth, they migrate north to the warmer waters of their breeding grounds. There is not much food there, so the adults must survive on their reserves of blubber until they are able to return to their feeding grounds.

MARCHING IN SINGLE FILE

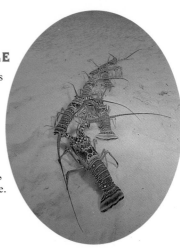

Spiny lobsters live close to the coast where the ocean bed is rocky. For most of the year they hide in crevices during the day, venturing out at night to feed on worms and dead animals. But in the autumn, along the Florida coast and the Caribbean, their behavior changes. They join together in long lines of up to 50 lobsters, each one keeping in touch with the lobster in front of it with its long antennae (*right*). They move off away from the coast into deep water, where they mate.

TURTLE TRAVELS

The green turtle (*below*) comes ashore to lay its eggs. But the turtles do not breed on any beach they come across. Instead, they travel hundreds, even thousands, of miles to the place where they hatched. Under cover of darkness, they haul themselves high up the beach, where they use their large, powerful flippers to dig a deep nest in the soft sand. After carefully covering the eggs with sand, the females return to the sea to leave the young to fend for themselves.

SPAWN AND YOUNG

MERMAID'S PURSE

"Mermaid's purses" – the dried-out, empty egg cases of skates, rays, and some sharks – are often found washed up on the beach. Here (*above*), a swell shark embryo sits on its egg case. The male fertilized the female, and when the eggs developed, she laid the egg cases, attaching them to seaweed by tendrils at each corner. The embryos live off the nurients in the yolk sac until they have developed enough to emerge.

Many marine animals do not have elaborate courtship behavior or care for their young. When the time is right, the female simply releases her eggs into the water, and the male fertilizes them with his sperm. The eggs are left to develop on their own. When they hatch, the young grow and develop without the help of their parents. However, the eggs and young are food for a great many animals. So hundreds, even thousands, of eggs are often laid by one animal in order that at least a few individuals survive to adulthood and are able to spawn (produce eggs) themselves. There are some exceptions to this rule. Like other mammals, whales are examples of animals that take good care of their young. When they are born, the calves are helped to the surface to take their first breath. They drink their mothers' milk for many months and are protected from predators by the adults.

DESPERATE DASH

Loggerhead turtle hatchlings head for the relative safety of the ocean (*right and below*). The mother loggerhead laid her eggs in the sand about two months earlier. As the babies emerge from the sand, it is the most dangerous part of their young lives, because they are easy prey for seabirds, crabs, and other predators. So as soon as they hatch, they scramble as fast as possible to the ocean. One day the females will return to the beach where they were born to lay eggs of their own.

BRAIN SPAWN

Coral reefs start when tiny planktonic larvae settle in warm, shallow water and become polyps. The larvae develop when a coral, such as this brain coral (*right*), releases packets of eggs and sperm into the water.

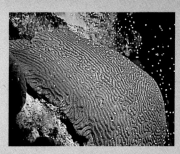

PUPPY LOVE

Not all fish lay eggs. Some sharks do lay eggs, but most sharks breed like whales and other mammals and give birth to live young. After mating with the male, the female carries an embryo that develops inside her body. When it is fully formed, she gives birth to the infant shark, which looks exactly like a very small adult. Here (*left*) a lemon shark pup is being born.

ROLE REVERSAL

Sea horses (*above*) do things differently: It is the male that becomes pregnant and gives birth to the young. The female lays her eggs in a pouch in the male's body, using a tube called an ovipositor, and then leaves him to look after them. Several weeks later the baby sea horses hatch and are ready to be born. The adult male then begins to convulse forward and backward, and with each backward movement a baby shoots out of the pouch. He gives birth to around 200 baby sea horses.

SOLE METAMORPHOSIS

When a sole is born it swims like other fish and has an eye on each side of its head (*below*). As it grows, one eye starts to move around its head, so that by the time it is an adult (*right*) both eyes are on the same side of its body and it is able to swim flat on the sea bed.

TEN DAYS OLD

THIRTEEN DAYS OLD

TWENTY-TWO DAYS OLD

ADULT SOLE

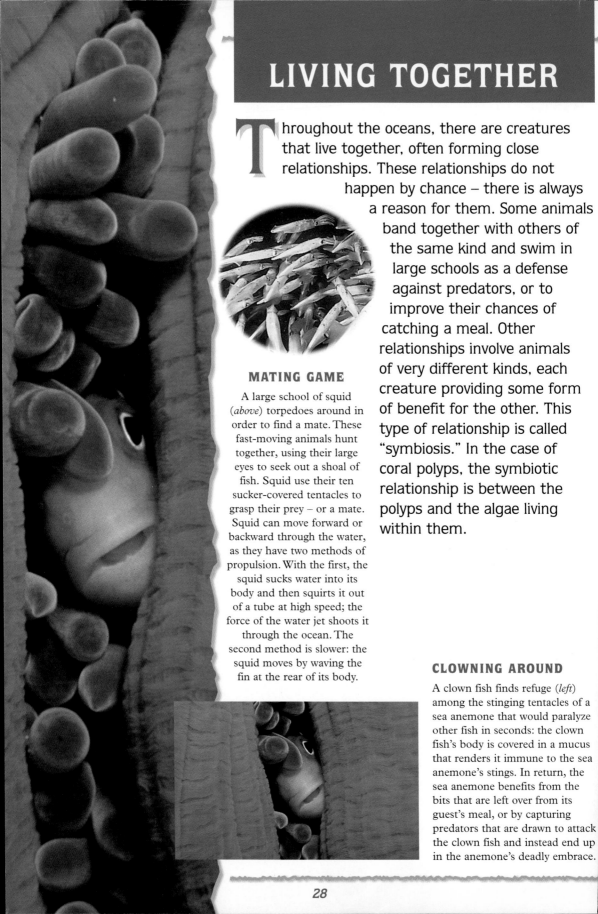

LIVING TOGETHER

Throughout the oceans, there are creatures that live together, often forming close relationships. These relationships do not happen by chance – there is always a reason for them. Some animals band together with others of the same kind and swim in large schools as a defense against predators, or to improve their chances of catching a meal. Other relationships involve animals of very different kinds, each creature providing some form of benefit for the other. This type of relationship is called "symbiosis." In the case of coral polyps, the symbiotic relationship is between the polyps and the algae living within them.

MATING GAME

A large school of squid (*above*) torpedoes around in order to find a mate. These fast-moving animals hunt together, using their large eyes to seek out a shoal of fish. Squid use their ten sucker-covered tentacles to grasp their prey – or a mate. Squid can move forward or backward through the water, as they have two methods of propulsion. With the first, the squid sucks water into its body and then squirts it out of a tube at high speed; the force of the water jet shoots it through the ocean. The second method is slower: the squid moves by waving the fin at the rear of its body.

CLOWNING AROUND

A clown fish finds refuge (*left*) among the stinging tentacles of a sea anemone that would paralyze other fish in seconds: the clown fish's body is covered in a mucus that renders it immune to the sea anemone's stings. In return, the sea anemone benefits from the bits that are left over from its guest's meal, or by capturing predators that are drawn to attack the clown fish and instead end up in the anemone's deadly embrace.

HAPPY HERMIT

This hermit crab crawls along the seabed (*right*). The shell in which it is living, and which protects its soft, vulnerable body, once belonged to a mollusk. On the shell it has placed anemones, whose stinging tentacles provide the hermit crab with protection against its predators. In return, the anemones get to feed on food particles left over from the crab's meals.

FLOATING FLOTSAM

Many different animals live among the floating sargassum weed and drift along with it, including sea slugs, crabs, shrimps, and goose barnacles, all cleverly adapted to their special habitat. Here (*left*) a small fish with fleshy growths blends in with the weed, making it almost invisible to predators. A sea anemone sits nearby, waiting for a fish to swim into its stinging tentacles. Both creatures are using color as camouflage, allowing them to blend in with the weed.

CLEANING SERVICE

Cleaner wrasses give the inside of a large cod's mouth a wash and brushup without being harmed (*right*). They help the cod (and other fish) by removing parasites or particles of food; in return they get a free meal.

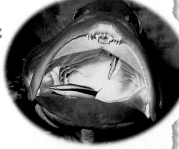

HITCHING A RIDE

A remora hitches a ride on a manta ray (*right*). The remora has a sucker on the top of its head which it uses to attach itself to the larger fish. Remoras are often seen on sharks, disengaging themselves to feed on the scraps of a kill.

PEOPLE AND THE OCEAN

TOURIST TRAP

A scuba diver admires the inhabitants of a coral reef (*above*). Foreign vacations in the sun are immensely popular, with many people visiting coastal or island destinations. Sun bathing, fishing, sailing, and diving are just a few of the popular activities available at resorts. While tourism brings the local population welcome money and a better standard of living, it also is accompanied by potential dangers for the environment.

People have always been involved with the oceans, depending on them at first for food and then later for mineral wealth. People have caught fish for thousands of years, and today fishing remains a major occupation in both the developing world and richer countries. Mining of the sea is important too. For example, the age-old extraction of salt from seawater has been joined by dredging of sand and gravel, and by drilling for oil and gas (*right*). Tourism has become a major industry too, and in many traditional coastal communities this has replaced fishing as the main source of income.

FISH HARVEST

This Scottish fishing boat (*left*) is bringing its catch aboard. Day and night, large fishing boats all round the world reap the bounty of the oceans in an attempt to satisfy the rising demand for fish. With more powerful boats, improved technology, and bigger nets, they are able to remain at sea for a longer time and bring home bigger catches. In order to avoid overfishing and depleting stocks of fish, there are international treaties that set precise limits on the size of a country's catch.

STILT FISHERMEN

In traditional societies
methods of fishing have not
changed in hundreds of years.
Here (*above*) a Sri Lankan
fisherman perches patiently
on his stilt while waiting for a
bite. For people in coastal
villages in poor countries, the
ocean is often the only source
of food. For many people it is
their livelihood, but often it is
under threat from foreign
fishing boats that take the
local fish stocks.

DIVING FOR PEARLS

A pearl diver in Thailand brings his catch of
oysters to the surface (*above*). The pearls are
formed around a foreign body, such as a grain
of sand, inside the shell of an oyster or mussel,
and take several years to grow. Pearl diving is
difficult and dangerous work. This diver is
using makeshift diving equipment made from a
generator and some rubber tubing. Pearls are
much valued as gems, and so the money the
diver earns from selling them makes the job
worth the risk.

PROTECTING THE REEFS AND OCEANS

U nfortunately, people often fail to realize the effect of their actions on the environment. This has been especially the case with the oceans, which, perhaps because they are so large, have been treated carelessly. Poisonous waste dumped at sea filters into the food chain, eventually affecting life at all levels of the oceans. Since the oceans have no real boundaries, the effects of harming them can spread well beyond the local environment. But increased public awareness of the issues has helped contribute to progress in protecting the oceans. For example, a United Nations-sponsored program promoting sustainable development in the 21st century, called Agenda 21, was agreed to by world leaders in 1992. This sets out key ways in which countries can, among other things, manage the marine environment.

WHALE WATCHING

Tourism has even reached the cold waters of the Southern Ocean. Here (*left*) a group of sightseers in an inflatable dinghy get a wonderful view of a humpback whale performing its aquabatics. Whale watching has become a popular form of tourism, but if it is left unregulated, there may be a danger that boat operations could interfere with the whales' everyday lives, especially during times of mating. If the whales feel harassed, they might abandon their traditional breeding sites, and that could spell disaster for the future of these majestic mammals.

TURTLE HATCHERY

In many countries, turtle eggs are a delicacy. On nights when the animals come ashore to breed, local people patrol the beaches and collect eggs for sale in the local markets. Some countries have tried to protect the eggs. In Sri Lanka (*right*), green turtle eggs are placed in a hatchery for protection, and baby turtles are released directly into the ocean.

PROTECTING THE REEFS

Some coral reefs have been made marine nature reserves, to protect them from overexploitation, such as the plundering of coral, sponges, and shells for sale to tourists, or the collection of fish for pet stores. People have found other ways of developing tourism in these places, creating local jobs without harming the delicate reef environment.

DOLPHIN DELIGHT

Despite being wild, bottlenose dolphins come into shallow water to seek human contact at the Monkey Mia resort in Western Australia (*right*). This interaction allows us to study wild dolphins, in hopes of understanding more about them. There are nearly 40 species of dolphin, but several are threatened by pollution, overfishing, and accidental death from being caught in nets used by fishing boats.

CLEANING UP

Pollution is a major threat to the marine environment (*left*). To tackle the problem, laws have been passed to ban tankers from cleaning out their tanks and dumping dangerous waste, such as radioactive waste, at sea. Measures are also being taken by many countries to reduce pollution from land-based sources, such as untreated sewage and toxic chemicals dumped into rivers that eventually flow into the oceans.

FOR FURTHER INFORMATION

The following are some of the sources available that can help you find out more about life in the ocean and about the protection of marine wildlife.

Books

Campbell, Andrew, and John Dawes (editors). *The New Encyclopedia of Aquatic Life* (Facts On File)
Day, Trevor. *Oceans*. Biomes of the Earth series (Facts on File)
Ferguson, Charlene (editor). *Are The World's Coral Reefs Threatened?* At Issue series (Greenhaven)
Luhr, James F. (editor). *Smithsonian Earth* (DK Publishing)
Ocean (DK Publishing)
Varilla, Mary (editor). *Scholastic Atlas Of Oceans* (Scholastic)
Walker, Pam, and Elaine Wood. *The Open Ocean*. Life in the Sea series (Facts on File)

Web sites

National Geographic Society www.nationalgeographic.com/seas/
Neptune's Web (U.S. Navy) pao.cnmoc.navy.mil/Educate/Neptune/student.htm
Ocean Conservancy www.oceanconservancy.org/
Ocean Link oceanlink.island.net/
Ocean World oceanworld.tamu.edu/
U.S. National Oceanic and Atmospheric Administration oceanexplorer.noaa.gov/

Publisher's note to educators and parents: Our editors have carefully reviewed these Web sites to ensure that they are suitable for children. Many Web sites change frequently, however, and we cannot guarantee that a site's future contents will continue to meet our high standards of quality and educational value. Be advised that children should be closely supervised whenever they access the Internet.

Museums and aquariums

Alaska SeaLife Center
301 Railway Avenue
Seward, AK 99664

American Museum of Natural History
Central Park West at 79th Street
New York, NY 10024

Aquarium of the Pacific
100 Aquarium Way
Long Beach, CA 90802

Bermuda Aquarium, Museum, and Zoo
40 North Shore Road
Flatts FL04
Bermuda

John G. Shedd Aquarium
1200 South Lake Shore Drive
Chicago, IL 60605

Mote Marine Laboratory Aquarium
1600 Ken Thompson Parkway
Sarasota, FL 34236

Mystic Aquarium and Institute for Exploration
55 Coogan Boulevard.
Mystic, CT 06355

National Aquarium in Baltimore
501 East Pratt Street
Baltimore, MD 21202

National Museum of Natural History
10th Street and Constitution Avenue, NW
Washington, DC 20560

The Seattle Aquarium
1483 Alaskan Way
Seattle, WA 98101

GLOSSARY

abyssal: referring to the deep ocean; much of the ocean bottom is an "abyssal plain"

algae: a group of simple plants that carry out photosynthesis and range from tiny microorganisms to huge seaweeds; the singular form of *algae* is *alga*

bacteria: a group of single-celled microorganisms that lack a distinct cell nucleus; the singular form of *bacteria* is *bacterium*

baleen: a substance forming comblike structures that occur in the mouths of certain types of whales, which use them to filter out food from seawater

bioluminescence: light produced by living beings

chemosynthesis: a process by which certain bacteria or similar microorganisms make food from chemicals; this process makes possible the existence of communities of organisms on the dark ocean bottom, where photosynthesis, powered by sunlight, is impossible

coral reef: an undersea structure in warm waters built over many years by simple organisms known as corals; the reef may rise as high as the surface of the water

mollusks: a group of animals that are invertebrates (lacking a backbone) and have a soft body, a muscular foot, and, in many cases, a hard shell; examples include clams, mussels, octopuses, slugs, snails, and squid

photophore: a light-producing organ found in certain marine creatures

photosynthesis: a sunlight-based process used by geeen plants and some microoorgnisms to make water and carbon dioxide into food

phytoplankton: planktonic organisms that are capable of photosynthesis, and so form the basis of most ocean food chains

plankton: tiny organisms – including plants, animals, and bacteria – found in a body of water

polyp: an individual coral organism or similar sessile invertebrate (a creature without a backbone) characterized by a cylinder-shaped body with tentacles

predator: an organism that kills other organisms for food

prey: a creature killed for food by a predator

sessile: referring to a creature that is attached to something and is not free to move

shoal: a large group, or "school," of marine creatures – such as a shoal, or school, of fish

spawn: eggs of water-dwelling creatures

tides: the twice-a-day rise and fall of water on a shore as a result of the gravitational attraction of the Moon and the Sun

tsunami: a large ocean wave produced by an underwater volcanic eruption, earthquake, or landslide

zooplankton: plankton consisting of animals

INDEX